Best wishes to Mary —
& all blessings
on you —

Carol Lynn
Pearson

A Widening View

Bookcraft, Inc.

Salt Lake City, Utah

A Widening View

Carol Lynn Pearson

Illustrated by Trevor Southey

Library of Congress
Catalog Card Number: 83-70994
ISBN O-88494-485-9

7th Printing, 1991

Lithographed in the
United States of America
Publishers Press
Salt Lake City, Utah

Acknowledgments

Acknowledgment is made as follows:

"The Laying On of Hands," previously published in the *Ensign*, August 1978.

"Real Tears," "Drama in Two Acts," "Trial Number Five," "From the Philosopher," "The Mother the Harbor," "Johnny's Shoes," "Joseph's Feast," and "Misunderstood," previously published in *This People*, Winter 1981.

Contents

A Widening View

When my eye first opened
Behind the viewfinder,
There, in closeup,
Was a flower—
The only possible flower.

Who turned the lens
For the pullback?
Life, I guess.
What—
Another flower?
And another?
A field alive with flowers.
(The only possible field?)

Loss.
Delight.

Borders are forever gone.
Life is at the lens.
The view goes on
And on.

The Little Trees

When she was small
She used to call
Them the little trees—
Those sapling cottonwoods,
A dozen or so
On the hill above the spring.

After a day's play with cousins
She would hear her mother
Calling from the door,
"Supper's almost done—
Come a runnin'."

And she would make
Her usual request:
"Please, Ma, can I walk them
To the little trees?
I'll run right back."

"All right. Hurry along."

So she would walk her cousins
To the little trees
And wave them on.

And then—
She was the one at the door,
That same door, calling,
"Time to come in now,
All of you,
Quick as a wink.
Tell your cousins good-bye."

"Please, Mother, can we walk them
Just to the big trees?
We'll go so fast."

She watched them
Walk their cousins
To the big trees—
Those blazing green cottonwoods,
A dozen or so
On the hill above the spring.

Rooted at the door
She watched them go.
And from somewhere
A wind blew through her—
The awesome thrill
Of things that grow.

The Mother the Harbor

These little boats
Came by currents
I may never know,
From oceans I cannot see
Even from my highest hill.

I cherish the cargo,
Bless the sea,
And thank the eternal itinerary
That harbored them awhile
In me.

Earth-Bound

That look on a little face
As a kite breaks loose,
As higher and higher
It floats and flaps—

That look,
Is it sadness for loss,
Or envy, perhaps?

Tug at your own string,
Little one.
When the wind is right
You will snap toward the sun.

To My Teenager

What do I do with a child
Who is taller than I?

How quickly you passed
My navel, my shoulder,
My chin, my nose.
And now there is
No more of me
To measure you by.
You are off the chart,
And it has thrown things
All askew.

How do you look up
To tell a person
What to do?

You can look down
And say,
"Hey, the radio
Goes off now."

Height
Means, "Now hear this!"
At least pulpits
And stands and stages
Assist in underlining,
Amplifying,
And being taken seriously.

I have lost my pulpit.
How can I preside?
Future shock is in my eyes
As I look up
And ask if you
Would be willing to
Turn down the radio,
Please?

The Nourisher

Without recipe,
Without dish,
You bring a banquet.

You step into a room,
Open, mix, bake and serve.
Instantly the feast is spread.

Instantly
I am fed.

For a Flawed Child

I would retouch you
Like a photograph
If I could,
Smooth you and tint you
Into glossy perfection.

But we are
Without a lab, my love,
And maybe I wouldn't
Do it anyway.

Some people get stuck
On surfaces, you know,
So satisfied
With the outside,
So thrilled with
The topmost layer of skin,
They're never moved
To move within.

I have glimpsed
What's in you, my darling,
And I wouldn't have you
Or anybody else
Miss it for anything.

16

Misunderstood

Ever since I,
A mere mortal mother,
Learned that there was
A better way than paddling,
Pinching, and pulling the ears—

I do believe
That God, grieved
By an erring daughter
Or a rebellious son,
Might use a variety of
Child guidance techniques.

But vengeance
Is not one.

Johnny's Shoes

He read the Johnny-sized words
And I read the big ones:

"Love your enemies,
Do good to them that hate you,
And pray for them
Which despitefully use you."

He knelt for evening prayer,
Pure as Johnny is always pure:

"Heavenly Father,
Thank you for the good day
That we've had.
And please bless the person
Who stole my shoes at the
Swimming pool today that he
Won't have to steal anymore,
And that he can have more
Love inside of him...."

Out the window
Or through the wall
(I wasn't quick enough to see)
Shot some small share
Of enormous wealth,
Never to be stolen,
Never to lose.

And somebody, somewhere
Instantly wore more than
Johnny's shoes.

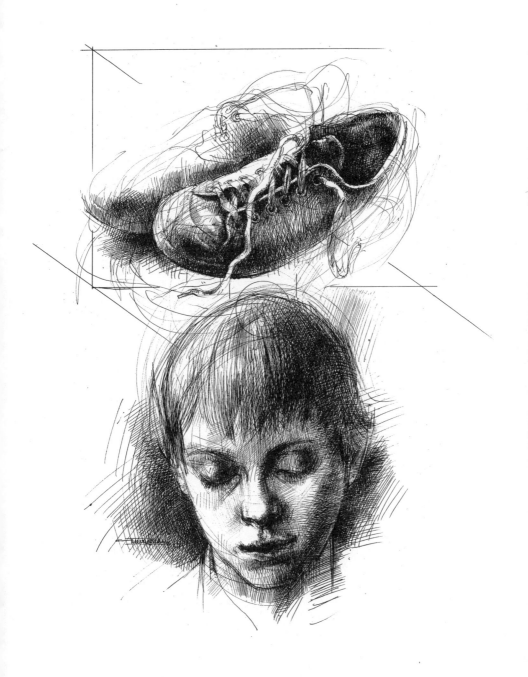

Urgent to Marilyn

Marilyn had a job—
Working out her salvation.
It wasn't nine to five.
It was nine to nine
In twenty-four-hour shifts.

And there was no vacation,
And in case she should get fired
Nobody else was hiring,
So Marilyn worked hard
And she worked fast
And she worked in fear.

The boss was away a lot
And Marilyn wondered
If he liked her work,
And not knowing, she worked harder.
She did everything on every list
Twice over to make sure.

She didn't have much fun
On the job.
It was more the retirement
Benefits she was there for,
The mansion, the glory.

On a typical day
She ran frantically
From the visual aid department
To the wheat-grinding
And quilting department
To the grow your own
Vegetables department
And the sew your own
Children's clothing department
And the physical fitness
Department.

She even stopped running
Past the genealogy department
And locked herself in
Until she got something done.

And then she ran
To the food storage department,
Ran with scriptures
On casette in hand,
Ran because there were
Twenty-two minutes left to fill,
Ran past the boss's memo
On the bulletin board:

"Urgent to Marilyn:
Peace, be still."

Laura and the Empty Tray

Sitting on the bench,
Waiting for the bus,
Laura looked like a person
Trying to look like the people
Who know where they're going.

Laura had been booted out of the house
By her husband,
Whose last words to her had been,
"I don't want to see you until five o'clock,
And don't you dare come home a minute sooner."
And then, almost pleadingly,
"Have a good time."

She had begged Stephen not to make her go,
Not to make her spend a whole
Eight hours out there
Doing anything she wanted to do.
She was already doing what she
Wanted to do, and she didn't have
Time for anything else.

"But honey," he had said,
"If there were *more* time,
If another whole day were magically
Tossed into the week—
A day just for you—
What would you want to do?"

Laura's answer came as quickly
As the computer prints item and price
In the grocery store:
"The downstairs bathroom," she said.

There had been two cans of paint
Beside the tub for months,
White eyes staring accusingly
At the walls that were slowly peeling
And at Laura, who was running in and out
Trying not to think
About the paint and the tube of calking
For the sink.

It was easy.
What would she do with another day?
The downstairs bathroom.

Stephen had taken her by the shoulders
And looked deep into her eyes
As if his own held a flashlight.
"Laura, where *are* you? Where are *you?*
I can't find the woman I love anymore.
She's lost. Help me find her."

Laura lowered her eyes and thought.
"Aren't we supposed to lose ourselves?
Isn't that what service is all about,
Forget yourself and serve others?"

"No," he said. "It's not.
You're supposed to serve everyone,
But you've been forgetting someone.
What can you serve from an empty tray?
How can you water plants from an empty pot?"

Laura started to cry.
When frustration began to well
Like the hot springs at her uncle's ranch,
She always cried.
He was right. She had been going on empty
For a long time.
She had been reaching into herself
As into an apron to throw feed
To a yardful of chickens,
And coming up with empty hands.
And the chickens cried louder
And sometimes she felt like wringing their necks
And sometimes like jumping over the fence
And running, running, running.

Stephen put his arms around her
And drew her close.
He hated to have her cry.
He would rather she yell or even hit.
But she always cried,
And hid in some dark corner inside
That no flashlight could find,
Making him stumble around in his search,
Palms out for blind man's bluff.
So he took her in his arms
and Stephen cried too,
Because he loved her.

"Look," he finally said,
Pulling her down beside him on the couch.
"Next Wednesday will be *your* day.
Go out—do anything you want to.
I'll hire a babysitter and get off early— "

"Pay?" she interrupted,
Looking at him like she looked at her children
When they suggested moving to Disneyland.

"A babysitter," he said quietly,
"Is cheaper than a psychiatrist."

Laura began to cry again.
He was talking about Donna,
A friend from where they used to live
Who they'd just learned had spent two months
In a psychiatric hospital.

How had it happened to her?
She had been the one who had done
Everything perfectly all the time
And done it with a smile—
Until she began kicking her children
And taking twice as much valium
As her doctor prescribed.

On Wednesday Laura was out of the house
By ten, telling the children
Something that was not quite a lie,
And giving the babysitter the
Longest possible list of things to do.

And now, sitting on the bench,
Waiting for the bus,
Laura looked at her watch.
Where in the world could she go
For a whole day?
If she had the children with her
They could go to the zoo—she'd been
Promising to take them to the zoo for months.

25

She looked at her watch again.
What if she went back to the house,
Climbed in the window downstairs
And did the bathroom?
No. Stephen would ask for a full report
And she couldn't lie.

Laura sighed, and the same feeling
Arose from the pit of her stomach
That comes with sitting in a traffic jam
When the dinner in the oven will be ruined
If it doesn't come out in fifteen minutes.

With everything she had to do—
Why—why did he make her—?

"I'll clean out my purse," she thought.
"I've been needing to clean out my purse."
Quick, efficient fingers emptied her bag,
Putting the good things in one pile
And the junk in another—
Sugarless gum wrappers, old grocery lists,
A petrified apple core,
The arm of a Barbie doll,
A program from last week's church service,
And a handful of cracker crumbs.

She threw the rubbish
In a garbage can by the bench and shook
Out the empty purse.
There, that felt better.
At least she'd have something
To show for her day.

Why hadn't she brought the bills?
Stephen would never have noticed
If she'd stuffed the bills and envelopes
And stamps into her purse—she could have
Paid all the bills.

The bus arrived and Laura boarded.
Maybe downtown something would come to her.

Looking out the window, Laura filed her nails.
Good thing she always carried
Her nail file around in her purse.
Then she did the eye exercises that
Once in a while she got around to doing.
Let's see. She didn't need a haircut.
Darn—if she'd brought her lists she could have
Gone to a phone booth and made her calls
For church and for the bake sale at school.

She looked at her watch again
And figured out what the babysitter had earned.
That feeling came again from her stomach
And she watched the babysitter's fee climb
Like you watch the meter at the gas station—
Fifteen cents—twenty cents—twenty-five cents.

The hot springs began to well again.
Why is he making me *do* this?
The bus passed the department store.
She could go in and get underwear
For Crissy, who had only two decent pair.
But Stephen had made her promise
If she bought anything it would be for her.

The bus stopped and Laura got off
And looked around
Like someone in a strange airport.
Maybe she should have saved the arm
Of the Barbie doll. Oh, well.
Let's see. She could buy some pantyhose.
That would be for her.
But if she saved the money
She wouldn't feel quite so bad about
The meter at home soaring higher and higher.

Two blocks away was the library.
Darn—why didn't she bring the book
She had found under the couch—
Bedtime for Frances.
She had paid for it already,
But maybe if she brought it back anyway
They would reimburse her—do they do that?
It wouldn't hurt to ask,
She had nothing else to do.

The walk to the library felt good.
It always felt good to walk with a purpose.
She opened the heavy door and was overcome,
As she always was, with the smell of the library—
That wonderful gluey smell that instantly catapulted
Her back into the excitement of adolescence
And school and learning
And looking at who else was there.
She'd always had to back in and out
Of library doors, for her arms were always loaded.

As Laura headed toward the desk
A display of paperbacks caught her eye.
To Kill a Mockingbird.

The title jumped out at her.
Just the other night she had driven
A group of high school girls home
From a volleyball game at the church
And they had been complaining about
Having to read *To Kill a Mockingbird*,
Thirty pages a day.

Laura had laughed.
"Oh, boy—I wish your English teacher
Would assign *me* to read
To Kill a Mockingbird.
Wouldn't I love to *have* to read
Thirty pages a day?"

Slowly Laura reached out and picked up the book.
A smile crept over her face and she looked around
Like you do when you find money on the ground.
Could she? Would it be okay?
Stephen *made* her come.
It wouldn't be *her* fault.

Laura chose a chair with cushions
And opened the book as guiltily
As if it had just come in the mail
In a plain brown wrapper.

At twelve o'clock she had not
Shifted once in her chair.
At one o'clock she shifted in her chair
But forgot the peanut butter sandwich
And banana in her purse.
At two o'clock she did not know that
She was in a chair—or a library—
Or a mortal body.

At 5:08 she closed the book
And stared at the wall for minutes,
Stared without seeing.
Suddenly she focused on the clock and jumped.
She was supposed to be home by five!

Quickly she put the book back on display
And then ran to the pay telephone by the door.

Her fingers easily found a coin
(Good thing she had cleaned her purse)
And she dialed her number.

"Hello?"
"Oh, Stephen, I'm so sorry.
I'll be home as soon as I can.
I came to the library to see
If they would reimburse me
For *Bedtime for Frances.*
But I forgot to ask them and I—
I read a book—I read a whole book, Stephen.
Stephen—are you there?"

"Laura?"
His voice was the voice you use
With your doctor after he has studied
All the tests.
"Laura? Did you have a good time?"

"Oh, yes. Oh, Stephen, it was wonderful!
I can't wait to tell you.
Oh, Stephen, thank you!"
Laura began to cry.

And Stephen cried too,
Because he loved her.

Laura had to back out of the library door,
For her arms were loaded.
Some of the books were for the children,
But some were for *her*!

She ran the two blocks to the bus,
Heavy—but not with books.
Full—like a tray, like a pot,
Full like a farmer's apron,
And she couldn't wait to throw it all
To the little chickens
And anybody else in the yard.

She had tomorrow all figured out.
Just think!—
A bathroom wall, then a book for the children,
Then a chapter for her, then a bathroom wall,
Then a book for the children,
Then a chapter for her.
And then, if she really felt like it—the sink.

Within

I read a map once
Saying the kingdom of God
Was within me,
But I never trusted
Such unlikely ground.

I went out.
I scoured schools
And libraries
And chapels and temples
And other people's eyes
And the skies and the rocks,
And I found treasures
From the kingdom's treasury,
But not the kingdom.

Finally,
I came in quiet
For a rest
And turned on the light.

And there,
Just like a surprise party,
Was all the smiling royalty,
King, Queen, court.

People have been
Locked up for less, I know.
But I tell you
Something marvelous
Is bordered by this skin:

I am a castle
And the kingdom of God
Is within.

On Going Back

Cry or threaten
Or bribe or beg—

A chicken cannot
Peck its way back
Into the egg.

To All Women Everywhere

Let us sing a lullaby
To the heads of state.

They are our little boys grown up
And they have forgotten the sound
Of their mother's voice,
And they need to be
Sat in the corner
Or given a good shaking.
Are they too big for that?

Then let us sing until their fingers
Fall from the fateful button
And they put the guns
And tanks back in the toy box
And remember that their mother
Told them we do not
Hurt one another.

Let us sing until they
Close their eyes
And dream a better dream.

Let us sing them to peace.

The Lighthouse

Do you know
How many count on you
To steer by this night?

Do you know
How dark the sea
And dim the stars
And strong the wind
Out there?

And you would
Hide your lighthouse
Under a bushel?

Don't you dare!

Pain

There comes a point
When pain shorts out.

An overloaded circuit takes
On charge after charge
Until
It brakes, shudders,
And is mercifully
Still.

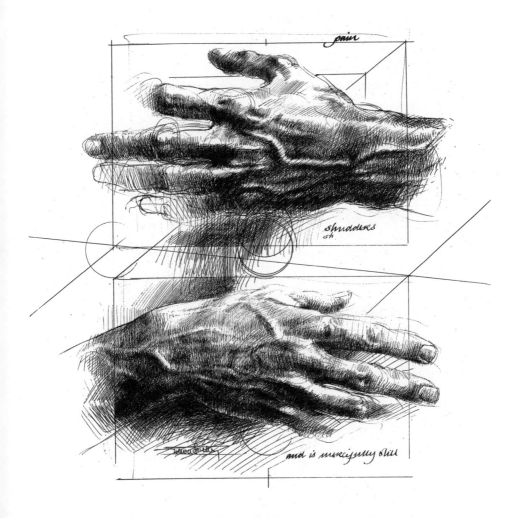

pain

shudders

and is mercifully still

Let Go

When you're giving birth,
Let go.

When you're watching at death,
Let go.

Whenever a life needs
A life apart,
Hold your heart.
Let go.

A Drama in Two Acts

I dim,
I dim—
I have no doubt
If someone blew—
I would go out.

I did not.
I must be brighter
Than I thought.

Alone

This is how I will die—
Alone
Like I am alone here on the beach.
Those who love me will stand back
Out of the wind
While I catch the current
That rarely takes more than
One at a time
And go.

I will come here
Every now and then.
I will stand on this spot,
Silent, blown.
I will practice being alone.

Miracle

To the unseen angel
Who holds to my breathing soul
The blessed anesthesia,
Much thanks.

I sense the surgery,
But do not feel it.
Stay close,
Until time can heal it.

The Days We Shared

They were generating days,
The days we shared,
Bright as when
Two fires combine.

I leave
Wearing some of your light,
As you leave
Wearing some of mine.

The Pearl

The little grain of sand
Is planted,
And an ancient urge
Begins its work.

I, the unhappy oyster,
Settle in the sea and curl
Defensive lustre after lustre
Around the pain—
Reluctantly
Pregnant with pearl.

Empathy

I,
Since split open,
Cannot contain.

I pour out
At the slightest
Sight of pain.

Labor

You have come in
Like a wounded animal
That crawls into a log
To die.

Now
Do not think me
Unfeeling.
It's just that I have
Been through it
So many times
And seen it
So many times
And know
I'll see it again.

I will hold your hand.
But if you see me
Smiling just a little
While you're writhing and torn,
Please understand
That I know labor pains
When I see them—

And frankly, I can't wait
To see what is struggling
To be born.

The Sunflower

Of course you have clouds.
What mortal sky does not?
Only in heaven
Are the heavens clear forever.

It's all right.
I am a sunflower.
I will find the light.

Connection

Incredible
That I have spent
All these seasons
Staring upward to see

How the tree
Fits the leaf
Instead of how
The leaf fits the tree.

Trial Number Five

Carefully they laid
Out on the table
Trials one, two, three,
Four, five and six.

"Choose one," they said.

"Oh, any," she cried, with a horror
Born of the best of Halloweens,
"Any but number five.
It would kill me.
I promise you I would not survive."

They thanked her graciously,
Escorted her out,
Then gift-wrapped, addressed,
And labeled "Special delivery"
Trial number five—

Sent with love from
Those whose assignment it is
To make sure you know
That you can go
Through trials one, two,
Three, four, ninety-nine,
Or five—
And, incredibly,
Come out alive.

Journal

Put the thought
In words
And the words in ink
In a page in a book
In a very private place
Like under a mattress.

A sacred process,
Wonderful as alchemy,
Is at work
Even in the dark
While you sleep,
Making something better
Than history:

Understanding.

Real Tears

When I played Joan of Arc
I cried real tears.

"Help me, Joan,"
Said the Bishop of Beauvais,
"I do not wish to burn you!"

That's when the tears would come,
Real tears on cue,
Every night for four nights.

When we struck the set
I saw them,
Little dry drops on the black canvas.
Strange, I couldn't feel a thing now,
But there they were.

I believe it will be
A little like that
When the current show closes.
When the set is struck
And the costumes cleared away,
I may drop by with a friend and say,

"Look—when I was playing Carol Lynn,
Back in space and in years,
There is the spot,
The very spot,
Where I cried real tears."

The Touch

Robert reached out
And took his father's hand.
His father didn't notice.
He had been in a coma for three days
And was not expected to notice things again.

Lying there, white against the white sheet,
He looked like a drawing that had been
Sketched but not colored in,
Except for the mustache and eyebrows
Done with a black crayon.

"Dad—"
Robert's voice was quiet.
His voice had always been
More quiet than his father's.

"Dad—I'm here.
I'm holding your hand.
You don't mind, do you?
All last night on the airplane
That's what I was thinking about—
Getting here in time to hold your hand
And say a few things.

Can you understand?
I know you can't speak,
But can you understand?
Maybe I'm talking more for me
Than for you anyway,
But that's okay.

Would you mind—if you were awake—
My touching you? I want to.
Why wouldn't you ever touch me?

I've got that picture of us
On my birthday when I was three
And you were holding me on your lap.
That must have been the last time,
Because except for a few spankings
And all the handshakes,
You hardly ever touched me again.
You even said 'Excuse me' if we happened
To brush in the hall.

Why did you have to shake my hand, Dad?
Why couldn't you ever hug me?
One time when I was over at David's house
His dad came in and kissed him
And he wasn't even going on a trip.
I must have looked amazed, because he said,
'What's the matter, Robert—haven't you seen
A man kiss his own son before?'
I hadn't.

Do you remember that I would never go out
To a real barber, Dad?
Do you know why?
Because once a month, when you gave me
A haircut in the kitchen—you touched me.
And it felt so good.

I think I was out of high school
Before I went to a real barber.
And since then we've had only handshakes, Dad.
I was so hungry—for so long.

Didn't you ever want to say 'I love you'
To anyone, Dad?
If you said it to Mom I didn't hear you,
And if you said it to me
I was asleep—or under three.

I guess you didn't think a real man
Did things like that.
I remember once when Mom was sick
And you did the dishes for her,
You pulled the blind down
So nobody would see.
And the time my best friend moved away
And I cried, you told me
To be a man about it.

Dad, I know I'm not the kind of man
You think a man ought to be.
I haven't gotten ahead like you wanted
Or made the money you thought I should.
Sometimes I cry, Dad.
And I even—Dad—I hug my little boys.
Even my big boy. And I kiss them.
It feels so good.

When you came to visit last Christmas
I wanted to put my arms around them
Right there in front of you—
But I couldn't.
And I wanted to put my arms around you.
But I couldn't.
So we shook hands and you left."

Robert stroked his father's arm.
"Dad—I used to blame you,
But I don't anymore.
You did what you knew.
And I do too.

That's why I prayed all night on the plane
That I'd get here—in time to touch you.
And to say—"

Robert stood and gathered the old man
In his arms and lifted him a little.

"Dad—I love you."
Then he kissed the old man's cheek
And his forehead and his lips.

Robert may have imagined it,
But he thought he felt a slight, slight pressure
From the white, white fingertips.

and lifted him a little

and lifted him a little

Coaching the Universe

I shout directions
To whoever is in charge,
As knowledgeably
As my own little
Backseat driver,
Age three.

From the Philosopher

Can it be,
In this huge
Hunger to know,

I try so hard to see backstage
I miss the best parts
Of the show?

Unpinned

I hope that humans
Never pin down
Love or God.

Things pinned down
(Like butterflies)
Lose something
(Like life).

I can go with progress.
I am grateful
For a long life span,
For medicine and computers,
And I'm glad to know
The layout of the
Galaxy.

But let some
Mysteries win.

Let love and God be free
As a million monarchs
To touch our faces
With bright wings
And leave wonder in our eyes
As they rise
From the hand-held pin.

Homemade

Woven on the little loom
Locked inside the inside room,
Spun to size without a seam,
Just the weight of last night's dream,
A shield against this morning's night,
Homemade, perfect—a garment of light.

Blessing

Spirit hands are on my head.
Father, Mother blessing me.
Comfort courses down like rain,
Cleansing and caressing me.

A Heavenly Message to One Who Has Never Had a Single Vision in His Whole Life

It's not that I have
Nothing to say to you—
It's just that I never shout
When a whisper will do.

The Laying On of Hands

Galaxies whirl within.
Little lightnings of love
Charge down arms,
Out palms.

A birthing is begun:
Warmth, sight,
And a gentle, private
Rising of the sun.

On Scott's Death

Another treasure
Has been transferred
To some foreign bank,
And I didn't even
Sign for it.

Withdrawals
Exceed deposits
And what am I to do?

Tellers,
I am at your mercy.
Somewhere between here
And poverty
Pay me to the order of.

Checked,
Stamped,
Cashed,
And then—

I shall be rich again!

Street-Corner Love

This is what I have
Against street-corner
Love:
It can't come in.

It stays on the skin
Until the next shower,
But it does not have power
To fill and flood
And set up residence.

I watch them walk
The dimly lighted places,
Empty eyes in empty faces
Crying "Come in!"

They cry "Come in!"
To one who can't.
Street-corner love
Is impotent.

The Grade

God does not grade
On the curve,
I'm sure of it.

But we sit around
Like high school students
In an important class,
Whose teacher has drawn
On the blackboard
The tiny wedges
For the A's and the E's
And the great bulge
For the C's.

We sigh in veiled relief
As the person down the row
Messes up,
Because it makes us
Look better
And probably means an E
For him, which is good,
Because while we have
Nothing against him personally
It means an A is more
Available to us.

And we secretly sorrow
When the person in front of us
Does really well,
Although we like her okay,
Because there goes another good grade,
Darn it, and we're looking
Worse and worse
And slipping further down the curve.

And God, I think,
Sits at the front of the class,
Holding A's enough for all,
Watching us
Work out our salvation
In fear and competition.

Getting Ready

He's always getting ready,
But never quite goes.
He's always taking notes,
But never quite knows.

He's touched by all the starving,
But doesn't touch his wife.
His life is spent at meetings,
But he never meets life.

The Prophet's Feast

He led us to the banquet,
He blessed the food, and then
Gladly he raised his fork
And the Prophet's feast began.

We watched in awe, and still
We stand with empty plate,
Sincere and hungry, testify
That the Prophet truly ate.

Homing

The windows are open.
Go as often as you please,
As far as you need.

Like the swallow
That flies
To Capistrano,
You will return
With homing
In your eyes.

Clear

I love you clear
As the crickets
Outside my window
On a clean, clean night.

There is no question.
They simply sing,
I simply hear.
And I simply love you
And know I love you
Clear.

Giving

I love giving blood.
Sometimes I walk in
Off the street
When no one has even asked
And roll up my sleeve.

I love lying on the table
Watching my blood flow
Through the scarlet tube
To fill the little bag
That bears no address.

I love the mystery
Of its destination.
It runs as easily
To child or woman or man,
Black or white,
Californian or Asian,
Methodist, Mormon,
Moslem or Jew.

Rain does too.
Rivers do.
I think God does.
We do not.

Our suspicious egos clot
On the journey
From "Us" to "Them."

So I give blood
To practice flowing,
Never knowing
Where it's going.
And glad.

Service

Who casts bread upon
The waters in crumbs
Receives it back
In loaves.

And who casts
The bread in loaves
Receives it back
In banquets.

Parent Friends

There will come a time
When these little ones
That come to me now
For bandaids and sandwiches
Will not need a mother much.
Already they are done with my womb
And done with my breast.

They will always need the rest
Of me, I believe—arms, heart, mind.
But someday I expect to find
That we walk with matching stride
And talk of things
That friends talk of.

Will there come a time,
Sometime after time is done,
Sometime when I no longer come to you,
Dear Father and Mother,
For bandaids and sandwiches,
Will there come a time
When we walk with matching stride
And speak our common, godly concerns?

Sometime, when this infancy ends,
Can we be
Not only parent and child,
But friends?